SEP   2019

W9-BDJ-876

THE NATIONAL
SEPTEMBER 11 MEMORIAL

by Ellis M. Reed

Cody Koala
An Imprint of Pop!
popbooksonline.com

abdopublishing.com
Published by Pop!, a division of ABDO, PO Box 398166, Minneapolis, Minnesota 55439. Copyright © 2019 by POP, LLC. International copyrights reserved in all countries. No part of this book may be reproduced in any form without written permission from the publisher. Pop!™ is a trademark and logo of POP, LLC.

Printed in the United States of America, North Mankato, Minnesota

042018
092018

THIS BOOK CONTAINS RECYCLED MATERIALS

Cover Photo: Alexey Filippov/Sputnik/AP Images
Interior Photos: Alexey Filippov/Sputnik/AP Images, 1; Shutterstock Images, 5, 10, 17, 19 (bottom left), 19 (bottom right); Red Line Editorial, 7; iStockphoto, 9, 13 (top), 13 (bottom left), 13 (bottom right), 14, 19 (top), 21

Editor: Meg Gaertner
Series Designer: Laura Mitchell

Library of Congress Control Number: 2017963476
Publisher's Cataloging-in-Publication Data
Names: Reed, Ellis M., author.
Title: The national September 11 memorial / by Ellis M. Reed.
Description: Minneapolis, Minnesota : Pop!, 2019. | Series: US symbols | Includes online resources and index.
Identifiers: ISBN 9781532160479 (lib.bdg.) | ISBN 9781532161599 (ebook) |
Subjects: LCSH: Memorials--New York (State)--Juvenile literature. | National September 11 Memorial & Museum (Organization)--Juvenile literature. | National monuments--Juvenile literature. | Emblems, National--Juvenile literature.
Classification: DDC 929.9--dc23

Hello! My name is

Cody Koala

Pop open this book and you'll find QR codes like this one, loaded with information, so you can learn even more!

Scan this code* and others like it while you read,

or visit the website below to make this book pop.

popbooksonline.com/the-national-september-11-memorial

*Scanning QR codes requires a web-enabled smart device with a QR code reader app and a camera.

Table of Contents

Chapter 1

September 11, 2001

On September 11, 2001, men **hijacked** four planes. The men crashed two planes into the Twin Towers in New York City. The buildings fell.

Watch a video here!

The men crashed the third plane into the Pentagon in Virginia. The Pentagon is the **headquarters** of the US military.

Passengers on the fourth plane fought back. That plane crashed in a field in Pennsylvania.

Chapter 2

Building a Memorial

Many people died on September 11. It was a sad day. But it also brought people together. Community members helped each other. People flew the US flag.

Learn more here!

Workers built a **memorial**. It opened ten years after the attack. The memorial stands where the Twin Towers used to be.

Chapter 3

The Memorial Plaza

The Memorial **Plaza** has

two beautiful waterfalls.

They flow into large pools.

The pools reflect the sky and

trees around them.

Learn more here!

Plaques are set around the edges of the pools. The plaques list the names of the people who died.

A pear tree grows at the memorial. It survived the plane crashes at the Twin Towers. It is called the Survivor Tree. Seeds from the Survivor Tree are given to places that need hope.

Charleston, South Carolina, received seeds after many people died in a church shooting.

Chapter 4

The Memorial Museum

The Memorial Museum has things that belonged to the people who died. There are pieces of metal from the Twin Towers.

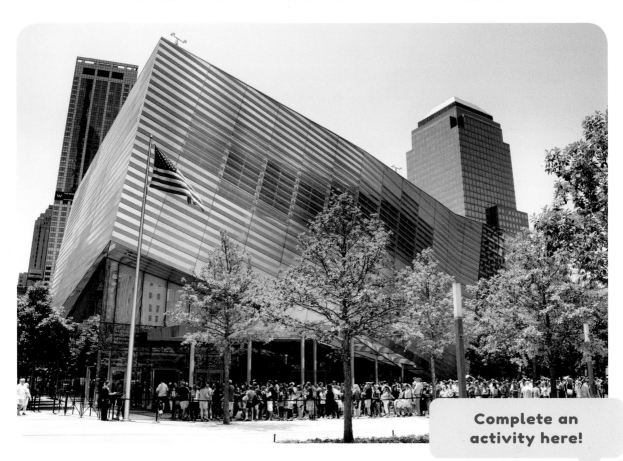

Complete an activity here!

The memorial is a symbol of community. It reminds visitors of the sad day.

Families who were affected by September 11 can visit the memorial for free.

But it also reminds them
of how people helped
each other.

Making Connections

Text-to-Self

Have you ever been to a memorial? What was it for? What did you learn about it?

Text-to-Text

What other books have you read about US symbols? What do the symbols tell us about the United States?

Text-to-World

The National September 11 Memorial is at the site of the original Twin Towers. Why do you think this is important?

Glossary

headquarters – the main location of something.

hijacked – took control of something illegally.

memorial – a statue or place set aside for remembering a person or event.

plaque – a sign that shows information.

plaza – a space outside that is open to everyone.

Index

Online Resources

popbooksonline.com

Thanks for reading this Cody Koala book!

Scan this code* and others like it in this book, or visit the website below to make this book pop!

popbooksonline.com/the-national-september-11-memorial

*Scanning QR codes requires a web-enabled smart device with a QR code reader app and a camera.